Undeniable Reasons To Go Vegan

Why You Should Change Your Ways

David Cook

ISBN: 978-1-7094-8543-5

Disclaimer:

This book is intentionally blank and does not list actual reasons to go Vegan. The material in this publication is of the nature of general comment only, and does not represent professional advice. It is not intended to provide specific guidance for particular circumstances and it should not be relied on as the basis for any decision to take action or not take action on any matter which it covers. Readers should obtain professional advice where appropriate, before making any such decision. To the maximum extent permitted by law, the author disclaim all responsibility and liability to any person, arising directly or indirectly from any person taking or not taking action based on the information in this publication.

DEDICATION

To the Vegans.

Printed in Great Britain
by Amazon

36508334R00113